GEOGRAPHY DETECTIVE

Mountains

Philip Sauvain

 Carolrhoda Books, Inc. / Minneapolis

All words that appear in **bold** are explained in the glossary that starts on page 30.

Photographs courtesy of: The Hutchison Library / Jeremy A.Horner 24t; / Melanie Friend 27; Impact Photos / Michael George 11c; Robert Harding Picture Library 14, 16t, 19t, 24bl; / F.Gohier 7t; Philip A.Sauvain 7b, 9t & b, 10, 11t & b, 12, 13, 15t, 16b, 19b, 22b, 24c & br, 15, 26t, 29bl, bc & br; South American Pictures / Tony Morrison - title page, 23t,c & b; Still Pictures / Daniel Dancer 26b; Zefa - 5, 8, 12, 15c & b, 18t & b, 20t & b, 21, 22t.

Illustrations by David Hogg. Maps by Gecko Limited.

This edition first published in the United States in 1996 by Carolrhoda Books, Inc.

All U.S. rights reserved. No part of this book may be reproduced, stored in a retrieval system, or transmitted in any form or by any means, electronic, mechanical, photocopying, recording, or otherwise, without the prior written permission of Carolrhoda Books, Inc., except for the inclusion of brief quotations in an acknowledged review.

A ZOË BOOK

Copyright © 1996 Zoë Books Limited. Originally produced in 1996 by Zoë Books Limited, Winchester, England.

Carolrhoda Books, Inc., c/o The Lerner Group
241 First Avenue North, Minneapolis, MN 55401

Library of Congress Cataloging-in-Publication Data

Sauvain, Philip Arthur.
   Mountains / Philip Sauvain; [illustrations by David Hogg]
     p. cm. — (Geography Detective)
   "A Zoë book" — T.p. verso.
   Includes index.
   Summary: A geological and geographic overview of mountains, their effect on humanity, and humanity's effect on them.
   ISBN 0-87614-999-9
    1. Mountains — Juvenile literature. [1. Mountains.] I. Hogg, David, 1943- ill. II. Title. III. Series.
GB512.S28 1996
551.4'32 — dc20   95-9525
                                                                               CIP
                                                                                AC

Printed in Italy by Grafedit SpA.
Bound in the United States of America
1 2 3 4 5 6 01 00 99 98 97 96

Contents

Mountains of the World	4
When Plates Collide	6
Rivers of Ice	8
The Remains of the Ice Age	10
Mountain Weather	12
From Valley Floor to Summit	14
Danger in the Mountains	16
Traveling in the Mountains	18
Using the Mountains	20
Mountain Farmers	22
Mountain Vacations	24
Damaging the Mountains	26
Mapwork	28
Glossary	30
Index	32

Mountains of the World

Most mountains lie close to one another in groups or long lines called mountain ranges or chains. They can be found on every continent. Some well-known mountain chains are the Sierra Nevada and the Appalachians in North America and the Apennines and the Carpathian Mountains in Europe.

- The highest mountain ranges in the world are the Himalaya, the Karakoram, the Pamirs, the Kunlun Shan, the Hindu Kush, and the Tien Shan. They are all in central Asia.
- Eight of the world's ten highest mountains, including Mount Everest, are in Nepal. Nepal is the world's highest country.

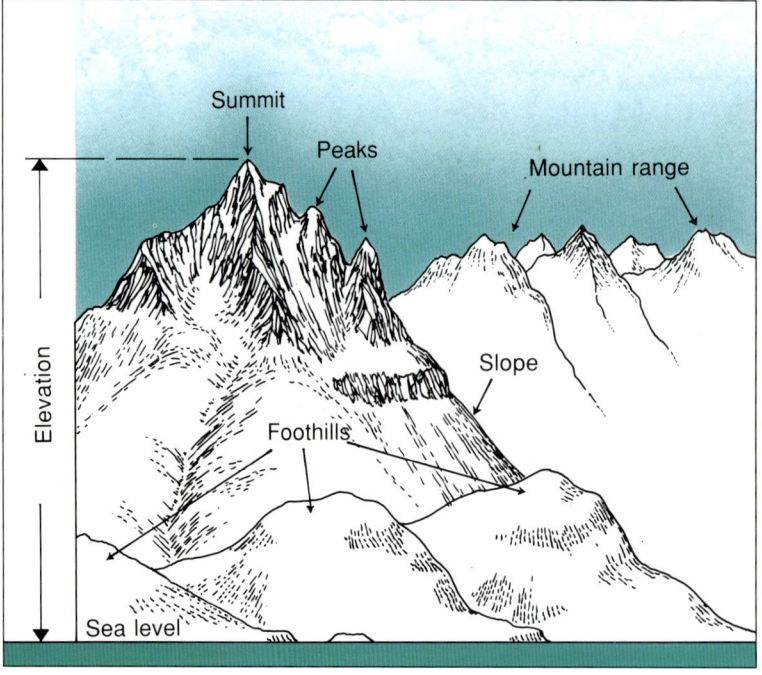

◀ This diagram shows some of the features of a mountain. We figure out the height, or elevation, of a mountain by measuring how many feet it is above **sea level**.

▶ This map shows the world's main mountain ranges. The diagram on the opposite page will help you compare the highest mountains in various regions of the world.

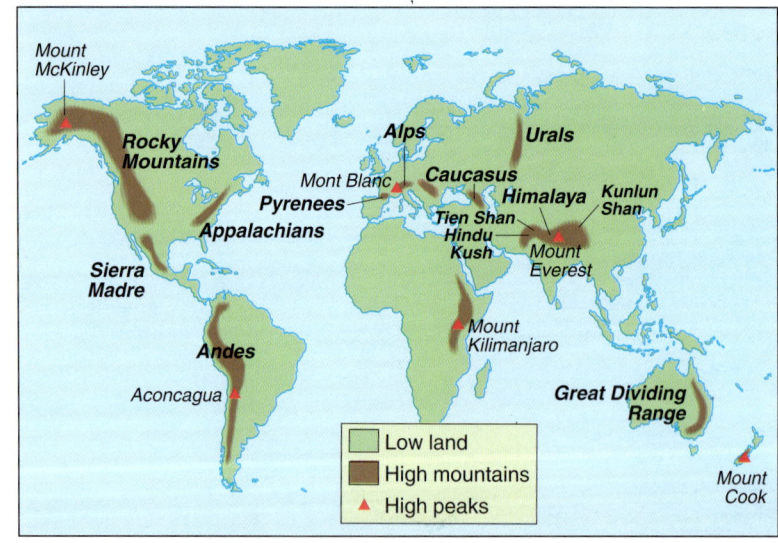

◀ Mount Everest lies in the Himalaya on the border between China and Nepal. It is the world's highest mountain. In 1953 two climbers became the first to reach the top, or summit, of Mount Everest. They were the New Zealand climber Sir Edmund Hillary and a Nepalese mountain guide named Tensing Norgay.

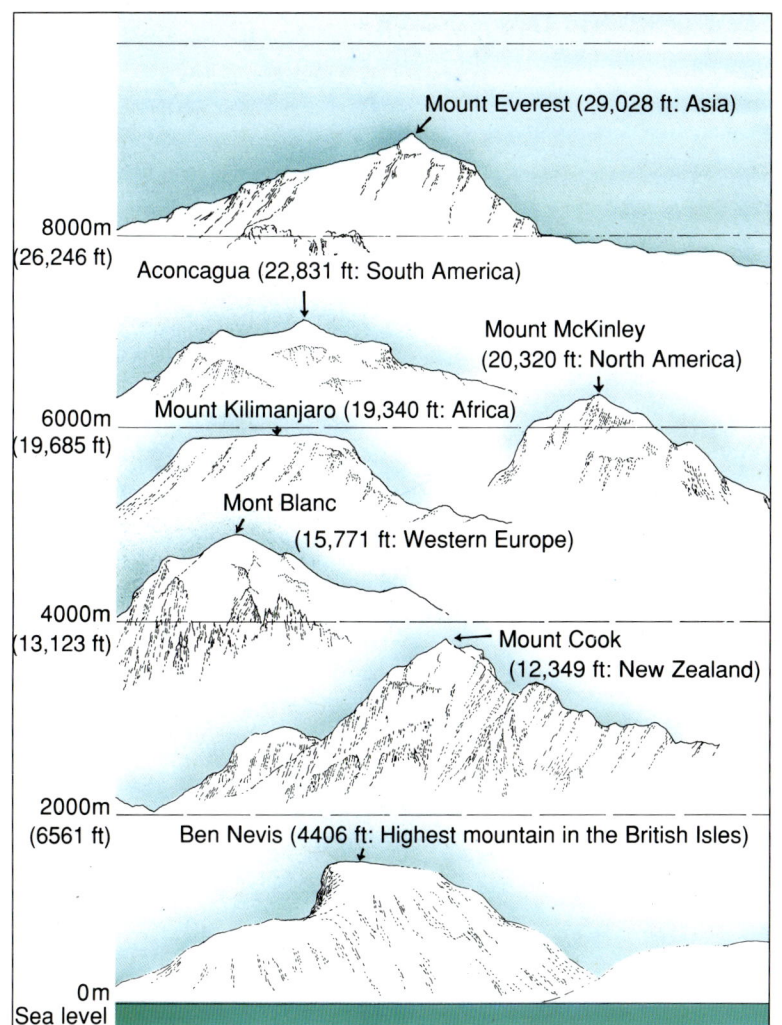

Geography Detective

Detectives use maps to try to find a pattern in the places where crimes have taken place. You can use the world map on page 4 to find patterns, too. Trace the highest mountains in North and South America. What pattern do they make? Look at the line of mountains from the Pyrenees in Europe to the Kunlun Shan in central Asia. Are they scattered, or do they form a chain? Which mountains stretch from north to south? Which stretch from west to east?

When Plates Collide

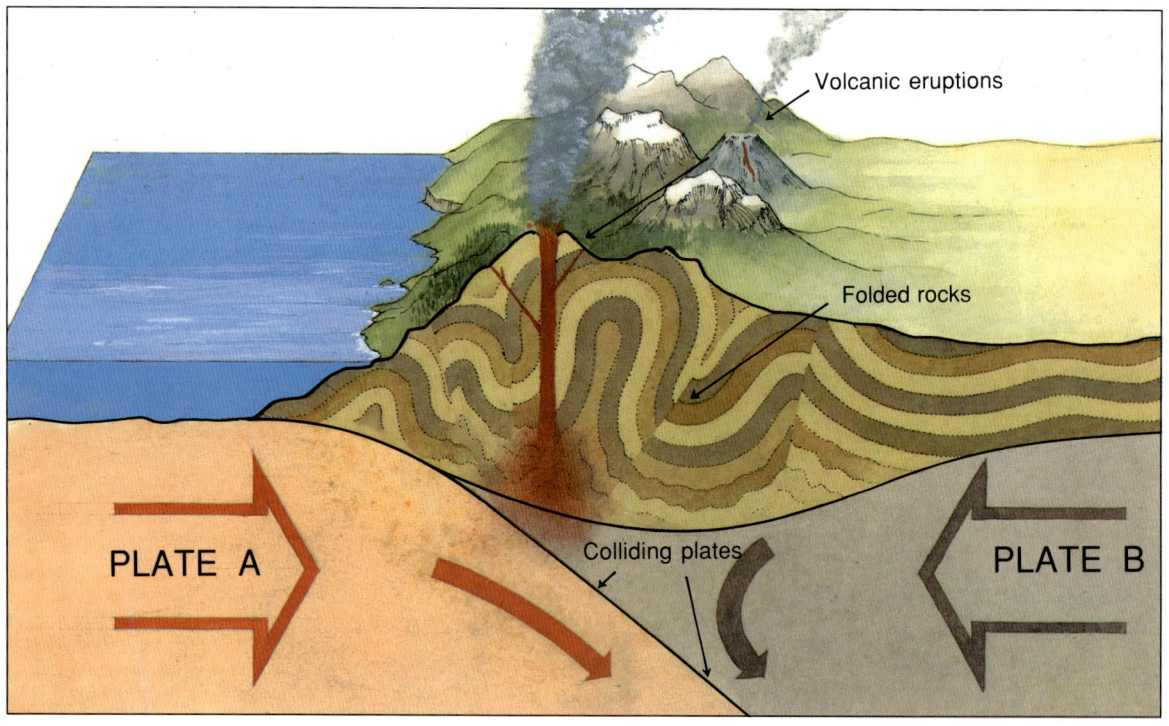

▲ When plates collide, the edge of one may ride over the other, pushing it down. Volcanic eruptions frequently occur as the plates rub against each other. Most new mountains are formed from this activity.

Most of the world's highest mountains are in two main chains. One chain stretches west to east from the Pyrenees and the Alps in Europe to the Himalaya and Kunlun Shan in Asia. The other chain stretches the length of North and South America from the Rockies in the northwest to the Andes in the south.

There is a reason for this pattern. The world's continents lie on **plates** — massive slabs of the earth's crust. These rock plates are moving. Some plates will shift their position by as much as six miles in the next million years. We cannot feel this movement, yet it pushes the edge of one plate into another, causing them to collide.

Over many thousands of years, plate movements force rocks to twist or bend, forming **fold mountains**. Along cracks, or **faults**, in the earth's crust, these movements can lead to **earthquakes** and **volcanic eruptions**.

● The world's highest active volcanoes are Guallatiri (19,882 ft), Lascar (19,652 ft), and Cotopaxi (19,347 ft) in the Andes of South America. Mauna Loa (13,677 ft) in Hawaii is the world's largest volcano, rising 30,000 feet from the ocean floor. Mount Etna (11,122 ft) in Italy is the highest volcano in Europe.

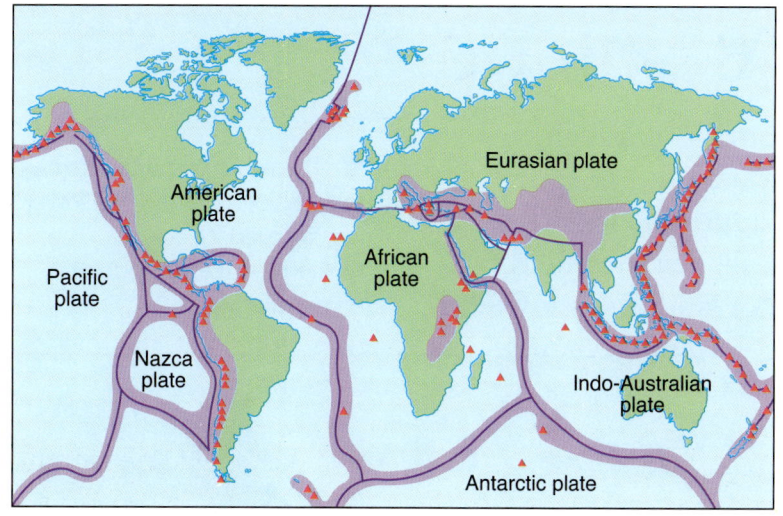

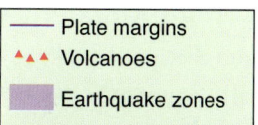
◀ Volcanoes, earthquake zones, and high mountains are found near places where plates collide.

— Plate margins
▲▲▲ Volcanoes
▓▓▓ Earthquake zones

Case Study

The map on page 4 shows the long line of mountains on the western edge of North and South America. These mountains lie close to the point where the Pacific and the American plates meet. This is why earthquakes and volcanoes are common along the Pacific coast. The San Andreas Fault stretches from northern to southern California. In 1906 an earthquake in San Francisco killed more than 400 people. An earthquake in Los Angeles in 1994 caused billions of dollars' worth of damage. Other signs of plate movements along the Pacific coast can be seen in the state of Washington. Here, the volcano Mount St. Helens erupted in 1980 and again in 1986.

▲ The San Andreas Fault in California is more than 700 miles long. It lies where the edge of the Pacific plate meets the American plate.

Geography Detective

What type of plate movement caused the feature shown in this photograph? Was it a crack, or fault, in the rocks on the earth's surface? Or did it happen when colliding plates folded rocks on the earth's surface? Have you ever seen rocks like this on a hillside, at the side of the road, in a valley, or along a coast?

7

Rivers of Ice

It is bitterly cold near the summit of a high mountain. Snow falls year-round and does not melt. Instead, it piles up and turns to ice. This blanket of ice and snow is called a snowfield. When it covers a large area of land, the snowfield is called an **ice sheet**. In time, the ice on a mountaintop begins to slide slowly downhill, forming a river of ice called a **glacier**. If the glacier moves over steep or bumpy land, the ice on the surface breaks into deep cracks called **crevasses**.

As the glacier moves, it scrapes away soil. It also carries stones and rocks that fall onto the ice from the valley sides. The tip of the glacier, or snout, begins to melt as it reaches the warmer weather lower down the mountain.

▼ These are some of the main features of a glacier. The lower half is called the tongue. The melting ice at the snout is called meltwater.

◀ This photograph shows the snout of the Mendenhall Glacier in Alaska.

- North America's longest glacier is Malaspina Glacier (90 mi) in Alaska. The longest glacier on mainland Europe is Jostedalsbreen (96 mi) in Norway. Much farther south, the longest glacier in the Himalaya, Hispar Glacier in Pakistan, is only 38 miles long.

- Arapaho Glacier in Colorado moves at a speed of about 20 feet a year. Alaska's Black Rapids Glacier was once 2,000 times faster. It traveled at an average speed of 115 feet a day!

◀ The crevasses on the surface of a glacier can be very dangerous to climbers. These cracks in the ice are sometimes more than 100 feet deep. Notice how dirt and rocks have darkened the color of the ice.

The soil and rocks that the glacier carries along are left on the ground when the ice melts. Single large rocks or boulders are called **erratics**. Mounds of dirt and smaller stones are called **moraines**.

▶ This picture of the Lauterbrunnen Valley in the Swiss Alps was painted in 1850.

Geography Detective

Look closely at the picture of the valley in the Swiss Alps. Notice the glacier in the distance. Then look at the same valley as it appears today in the photograph on page 10. What has changed? Draw two sketches to show what happened. What does this tell you about the weather in the Swiss Alps in the last 150 years?

The Remains of the Ice Age

Thousands of years ago, much of Europe and North America were covered by ice. This period of time is called the **Ice Age**. Since then, warmer weather has melted most of the ice. It has left behind many features that were formed by glaciers or ice sheets. You have to be a geography detective to find these features today! You can see some of them in the photographs. These features are clues to the past.

◀ Glaciers carve out what are called **U-shaped valleys**, because they look like the letter U. The smaller valleys leading into the main valley were left "hanging" when the glacier deepened the main valley. These side valleys are called **hanging valleys**. Streams often plunge from hanging valleys into lower valleys, forming waterfalls.

◀ Sometimes a glacier hollows out the side of a mountain, near the summit. Called **cirques**, these hollows are formed over thousands of years, as the ice grinds against the mountainside.

● Ice ages are periods when ice sheets and glaciers cover large areas of the earth's continents. There have been several ice ages, with warmer weather in between. The last Ice Age ended about 10,000 years ago.

● Some valleys have been deepened by a glacier or blocked at one end by a moraine. Long, narrow stretches of water called **finger lakes** are often found in these valleys.

◀ This rock is in Central Park in New York City. Called an erratic, the rock was moved here by ice thousands of years ago. Clues like this tell us that an ice sheet once covered most of North America. Scientists called geologists can tell which mountains the rock came from.

Geography Detective

A glacier drags sharp stones along the bare rock of a valley floor. These stones cut deep scratches in the floor. The scratches are called **striations**. How do striations help us know the direction in which glaciers move? How do erratics help us know how far glaciers travel? Imagine that you are standing in a U-shaped valley. What clues will you look for to tell you that a glacier has been there?

11

Mountain Weather

The higher you climb, the colder and wetter the weather gets. This is why you need warm clothing and rain gear when you climb a mountain. It also explains why Africa's Mount Kilimanjaro and Mount Kenya have snow and ice, even though both mountains are close to the **equator**, where the weather is hot all year.

▼ The weather in the mountains affects how people use the land. In this mountain valley, the weather is colder and wetter than in the nearby lowlands. The valley is more exposed to winds and more likely to be in the shade during the day.

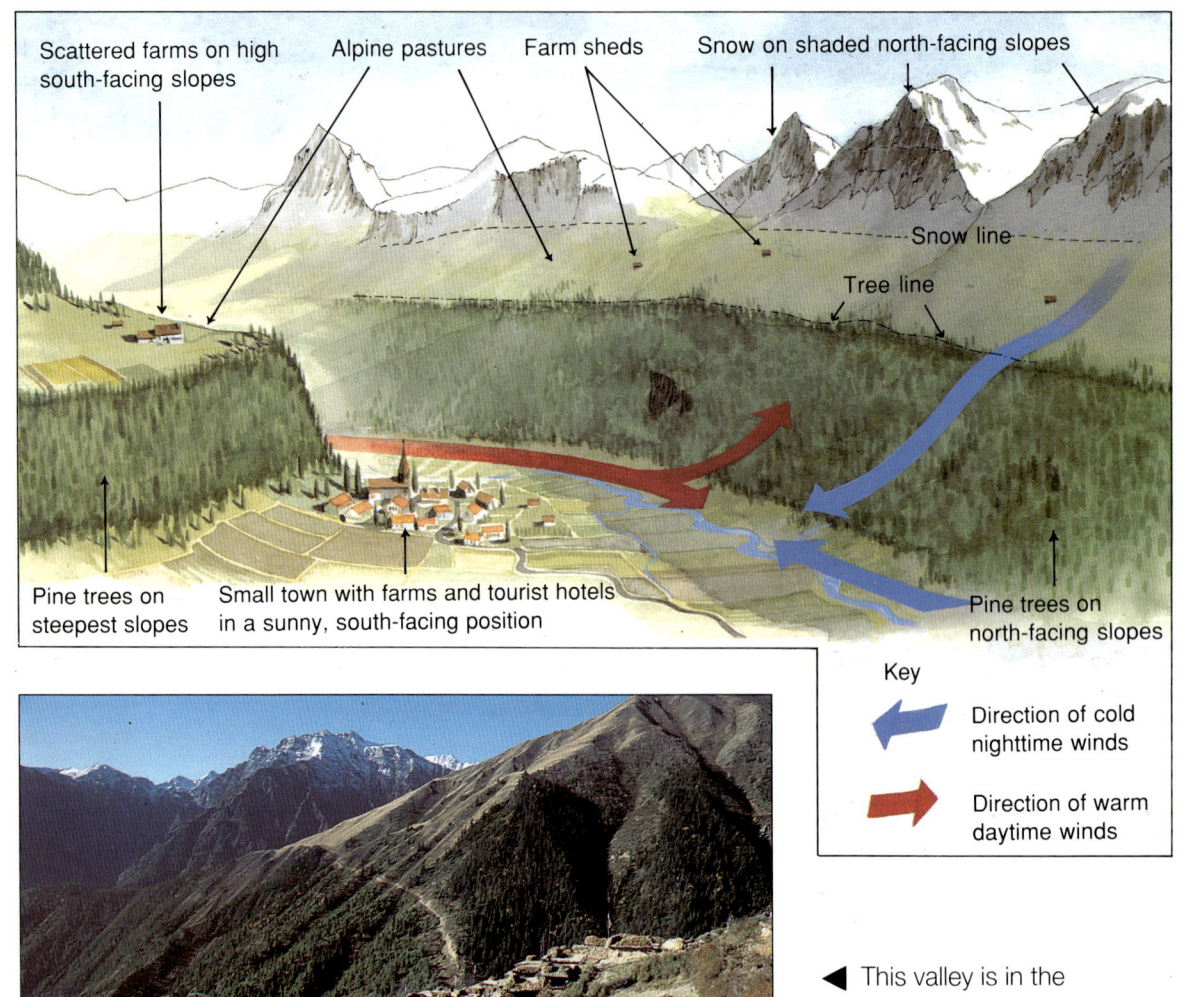

◀ This valley is in the Himalaya. People who live in mountain valleys usually build their homes on the side that faces the most sunshine. The slopes on the other side of the valley are in the shade for most of the day.

Too much rain and wind is bad for many crops, and frost can kill delicate plants. Crops and plants that need a lot of warmth and sunshine to ripen grow lower down the mountain.

Cone-bearing evergreen trees can survive up to the **tree line**. Beyond this line the weather is too cold for any trees to grow. Grass will grow above the treeline, but not above the **snow line**. Beyond the snow line, snow and ice cover the ground all year.

◀ The style of this wooden chalet in the Alps tells us something about the weather there. The edge of the roof sticks out beyond the walls to protect people below when snow slides off the sloping roof.

Geography Detective

This diagram shows how the temperature changes during a cable car ride up a mountain. What difference in elevation is there between the place where the journey started and the place where it ended? How many degrees colder is it at the top than at the bottom? How many degrees does the temperature fall for each 1,000 feet in height? How high up the mountain would you be when the temperature reached the freezing point (32°F)?

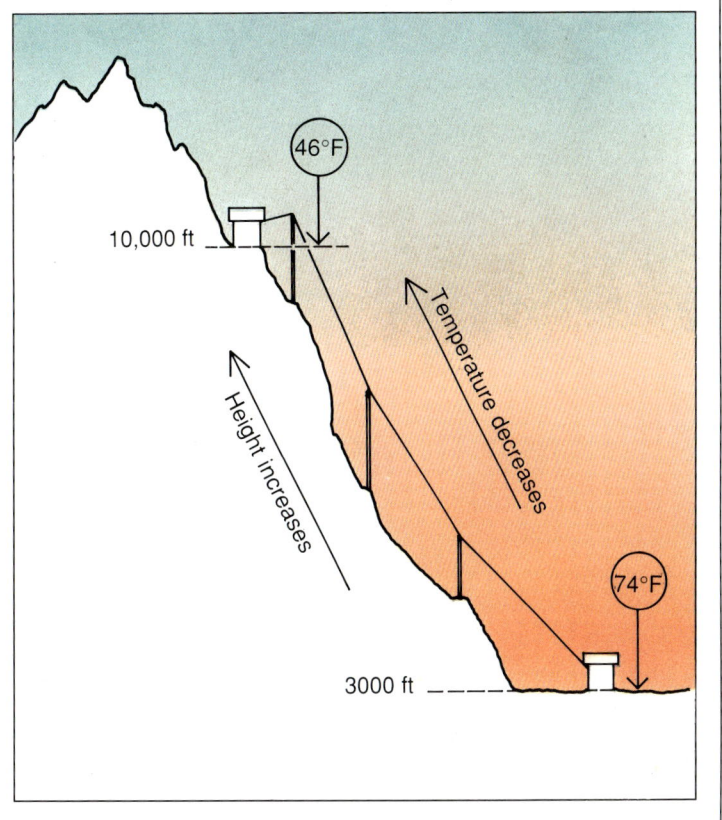

From Valley Floor to Summit

Different types of trees, flowers, grasses, and other plants grow at specific elevations on a mountain slope. Animals and birds feed on certain plants or on creatures that eat certain plants. So different animals and birds will also live at different elevations on the mountain.

- The temperature at the summit of a mountain depends on two things — its elevation above sea level and how close it is to the North Pole or the South Pole. A mountain that is 6,500 feet high always has snow cover in Norway but not in Spain, which is much closer to the equator.
- Still closer to the equator, Mexico City lies at 7,347 feet above sea level, yet flowers bloom year-round.

▶ This diagram shows the types of plants and crops at various elevations in the Himalaya.

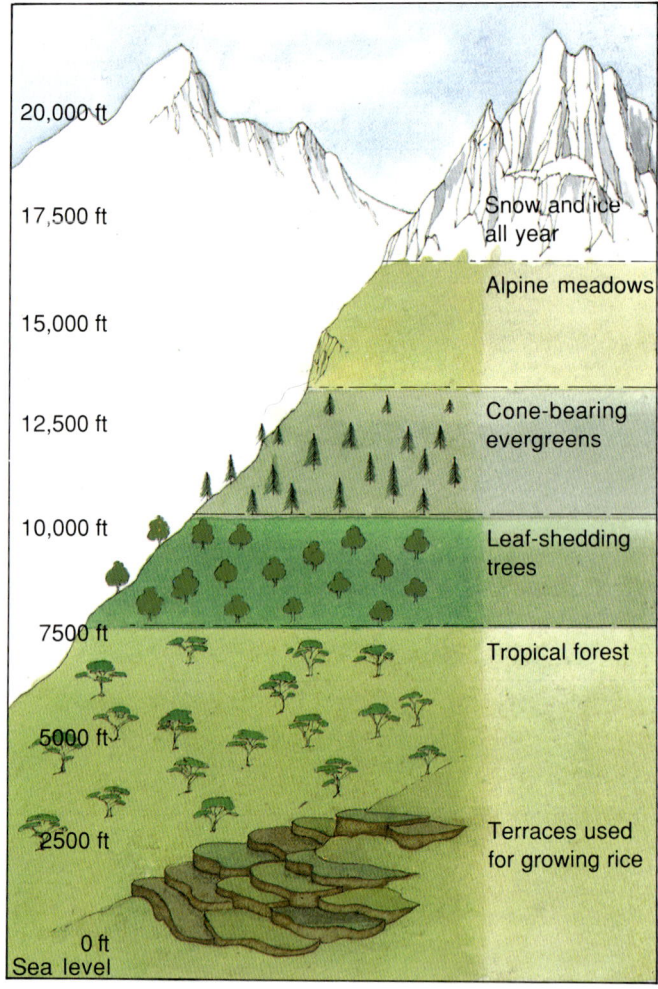

◀ Wild animals and birds live in the hot tropical grasslands of eastern Africa. These plains lie at the foot of Mount Kilimanjaro in Kenya. Kilimanjaro (19,340 ft) is Africa's highest mountain. Even though it is very close to the equator, the summit has snow and ice all year.

The plants and animals that live in the mountains have become used to the weather there. The mountain hare and the ptarmigan both turn white in winter. Small, low-growing mountain flowers, called **Alpines**, grow in the thin rocky soil. They spend the winter under a thick blanket of snow. In summer they seek light and warmth. Notice how the trumpets of the Alpine gentian are leaning toward the sun.

▲ Alpine gentian

▲ Snowshoe hare ▼ Willow ptarmigan

Geography Detective

Look at the photographs. Why do mountain creatures such as the ptarmigan and the mountain hare change color from brown to white with the seasons? Why do Alpine flowers grow close to the ground? What would happen to tall plants in the winter? Find other ways in which mountain animals and plants tell you something about the cold weather and the rocky landscape.

15

Danger in the Mountains

◀ A sudden rush of falling snow and rock is called an **avalanche**. This is one of the greatest dangers to climbers and skiers.

Mountains are dangerous places for people who are not properly dressed or equipped. Mountain weather is difficult to predict. Hot, calm, clear, sunny weather in the morning can soon turn into driving rain, biting winds, heavy snow, or dense fog. Even expert climbers can lose their way when landmarks are blotted out by poor weather. This is why sensible travelers wear strong boots and waterproof clothing. They carry ice axes, maps, and a compass. They also carry chocolate as emergency food, in case they have to spend the night on the mountain.

● About 100,000 avalanches a year happen in the mountains of the western United States. Just a slight vibration or the added weight of new snow can trigger a disaster.

● Some of the worst avalanches have happened in the Andes of Peru. In 1962 a huge mass of ice and snow tumbled down Mount Huascaran. In just 15 minutes, the avalanche wiped out six villages and killed 3,500 people. In 1970 falling rock and ice killed 18,000 people and destroyed the town of Yungay, Peru.

◀ Look at the deep snow near the summit of this mountain. The snow may be hanging over the edge of a cliff, or a bridge of snow may be covering a crevasse. The surface of the rock beneath the snow might be very slippery. These are some of the hidden dangers that threaten climbers.

Avalanche danger: run closed to skiers (North American sign)

Avalanche danger: run closed to skiers (European sign)

◀ Signs warn skiers of avalanche conditions. If you see these signs, you should keep away.

People who live in the mountains are prepared for avalanches and heavy snowfalls. Mountain dwellers have several ways of protecting themselves from danger.

▼ Snow fences stop snowdrifts from blocking mountain roads. The fences are made from strips of wood to let the wind blow through without carrying snow. Long wooden shelters called **snowsheds** keep snow from piling up on mountain railways. The snowsheds also protect passengers if there is a sudden avalanche.

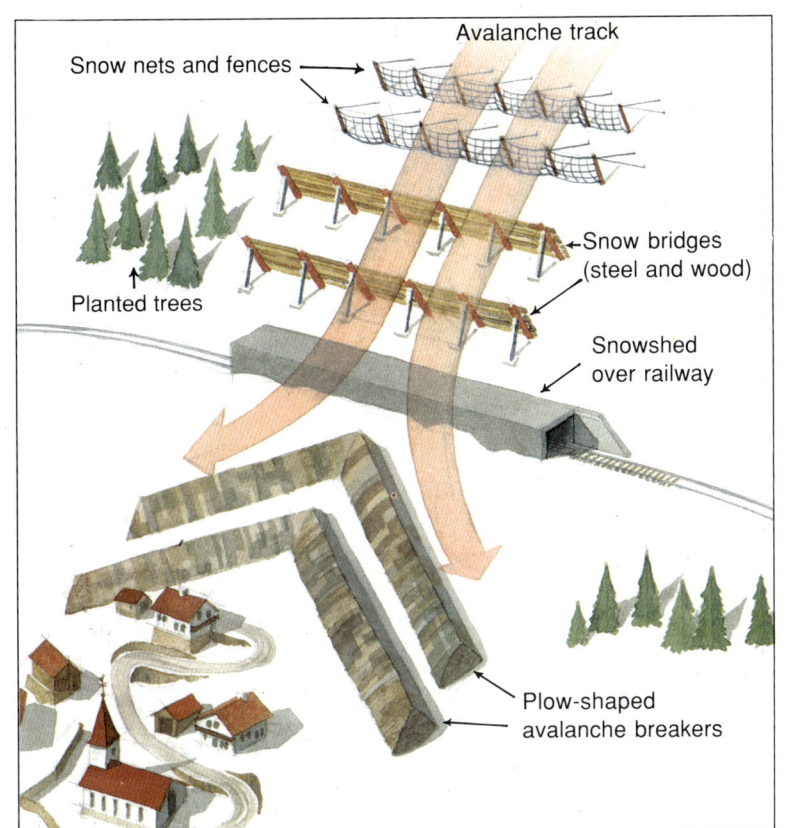

Geography Detective

This picture shows some ways that avalanches can be prevented. It also shows how to keep an avalanche from causing too much damage. How does each method work? Just one skier can start an avalanche. What else do you think might start one?

Traveling in the Mountains

◀ People living in the Himalaya use mules and yaks to carry heavy loads. Few roads exist in the high mountains. Only surefooted animals can make their way easily over mountain trails like this.

The first travelers in the highlands went on foot and carried their own baggage. Later, people used pack animals like those in the photograph. Today, railways and paved roads have been built in many mountain areas. The railways and paved roads that cross the Rockies, the Alps, and other mountains link towns and cities on either side. They take the quickest and easiest routes. By following river valleys and lakeshores, roads and railways are made as straight and as level as possible. Tunnels and bridges also help shorten the route.

Roads and railways in the mountains are built for tourists and for people who live and work in the region. Some narrow mountain railways are used to bring food and other goods to isolated towns and villages. These trains are specially built to climb steep slopes even when the tracks are covered with snow. The diagram on page 19 shows how they do this.

- The highest railway station in the world is in the Andes, at Condor in Bolivia. It is almost 16,000 feet above sea level.
- The world's highest paved road crosses Xizang (Tibet) in China. It is more than 18,000 feet above sea level.

▼ This train is traveling through the Rocky Mountains in Canada. Notice how the railroad follows the curve of the valley.

◀ Mountain roads, such as this one in Greece, often zigzag up steep slopes. The zigzags, called switchbacks, are easier for vehicles to climb. Switchbacks make the slope, or **gradient**, from bend to bend much less than it would be if the road were straight. In winter these roads can be very slick. Some drivers fit snow chains over their tires to grip the icy surface.

Geography Detective

The photograph and the diagram show two ways of getting a railway up a steep slope. Can you see how they work? What would you expect to see underneath the trains that use the railway track in the photograph? Look at the diagram. The place where the railway tracks meet is called a junction. Why do you think these are called Y-junctions?

▼ Y-junctions in the Andes   ▲ Mountain railway in the Alps

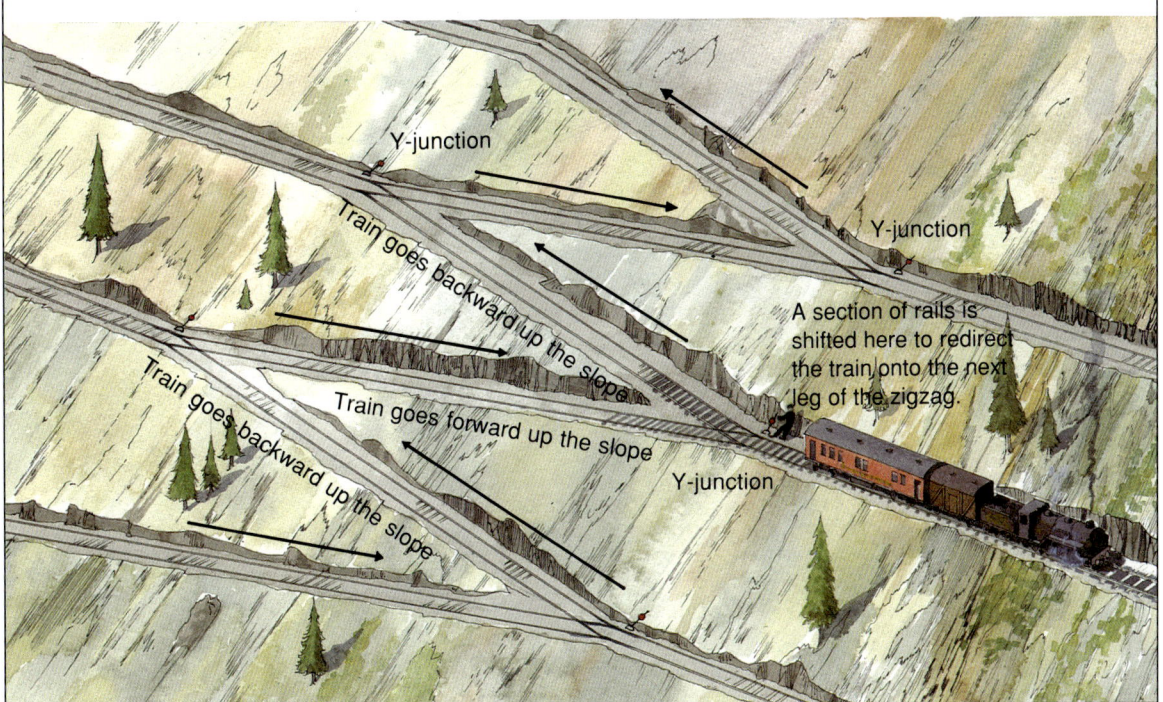

Using the Mountains

◀ Some mountains contain copper and other minerals in the rocks. This huge copper mine is at Bingham Canyon in the Rocky Mountains of Utah. A mine like this provides jobs for people living nearby. But mining activities also change the landscape.

Many people in the mountains earn their living from natural resources. They may farm the soil, mine rocks, or cut logs. The most important natural resource today is the beauty of the mountains. Tourists come to view the scenery, to hike or ski, to fish or raft the rivers. Tourism (see pages 24–25) provides thousands of jobs for local people. Without a way to earn a living, people would be unable to live in mountain areas.

● Mountain slopes are often too shaded and too steep for anything other than trees to grow there. Tree roots help stop the soil from being washed away. If they are properly cared for, forests are a valuable natural resource for logging and for tourism. Each year forestry workers plant trees to replace those they cut down.

◀ In many mountain areas, such as North America's Pacific Northwest, logging, or forestry, is a very important industry. At local sawmills, the logs are cut into boards used in construction. In other places, woodcarving is a major craft. The mountains of southern Germany are famous for cuckoo clocks and for musical instruments.

Water is another useful resource in the mountains. The main sources of water are heavy rainfall and melting glaciers, ice, and snow. Sometimes a mountain river is dammed so that the water collects and forms a lake, or **reservoir**. The reservoir stores fresh water for cities. The water is also used to turn machines called turbines. They help make **hydropower**, a form of electricity that is cheap and clean because it does not burn fuel. In mountainous regions, industries rely on hydropower to fuel their machinery.

● When dams are built, their reservoirs flood valleys and destroy plants and wildlife. New roads to a dam may spoil beautiful scenery. Dams also block the travel and feeding patterns of fish and other wildlife.

◀ This dam across the Gordon River in Australia is part of a hydropower project.

Geography Detective

People who live in the mountains need jobs. Yet the mountains and valleys where they live are easily spoiled. Make a list of the ways in which the activities shown here could harm a mountain.

Mountain Farmers

◀ These farmers live on the lower slopes, or **foothills**, of the Himalaya. They have created flat fields called terraces by cutting "steps" into the hillsides. The terraces help prevent **erosion**, so that wind and rain will not carry fertile soil down the slopes.

Farmers have a hard time farming in the mountains. Above the valleys, there is not much land suitable for growing crops. Mountain fields are often too small and too steep for tractors and other machines. Mountain soil is also thin and rocky. The period of the year when there is enough light and warmth for plants to grow — called the growing season — may be very short in mountain areas.

Yaks, mountain goats, sheep, and llamas are animals that can survive outside in a cold winter. Most high land is suitable only for grazing these hardy animals. Cattle are kept inside in winter.

● The mountain farmers of the Andes are used to their harsh environment. The air is much thinner at high altitudes, so most of the people there have larger lungs than people who live down lower. Larger lungs make it easier to breathe the thin air.

● Mountain animals, such as sheep and llamas, can move around easily on high pastures. Their small feet help them grip the steep slopes and bare rock.

◀ Many mountain farmers take their cattle, goats, and sheep up the mountains each summer. The animals graze on the new grass that grows on the slopes above the tree line. The farmers take the animals down the mountain again each autumn to protect them from winter cold. This movement of livestock each year is called **transhumance**.

They graze on the high pastures in summer, when the grass is fresh and green. Dairy products are often made in mountain areas. Fresh milk is turned into butter, cheese, or cream in the farmhouse, or in a creamery. These products are then sold in cities.

Case Study

The people of the Andes have learned how to make the best possible use of their mountain pastures. They graze their sheep and llamas and grow a few crops in the thin mountain soil. They bring their products to market in the small hill towns. Life has changed little here for hundreds of years.

Geography Detective

What mountains are nearest to your home? Find some pictures of these mountains. What types of farming do you see there? What crops do the farmers grow? What animals are grazing on the slopes? How does the farming affect the landscape?

▼ These scenes show everyday life in the Andes Mountains of Peru.

Mountain Vacations

Throughout the world, people enjoy mountains for recreation and for vacation. In winter, many mountain villages become ski resorts. The best ski resorts have plenty of winter snow.

▼ These skiers are riding a ski lift in Breckenridge, a ski resort in the Colorado Rockies.

◀ From this base camp in Kumbu, Nepal, climbers will try to reach the top of Mount Everest. Many people like the challenge and risk involved in rock climbing. They enjoy testing their limits as they scale a steep rock face.

▲ Hang gliding

Hang gliding and hot-air ballooning are popular in some mountain valleys. The flyers use warm air currents that rise from the valley floor to keep their craft in the air.

▼ Hot-air ballooning

◀ This is the main street in Chamonix, which is one of the most famous resorts in France. Tourists come here to hike, to ski, and to view Mont Blanc. You can see Mont Blanc in this photograph. It is the highest mountain in western Europe.

● In 1924 Chamonix became the first ski resort to host the Winter Olympics. Since then, many ski resorts have staged the Winter Olympics. Among these resorts are Lillehammer in Norway in 1994, Albertville in France in 1992, Calgary in Canada in 1988, Sarajevo in Bosnia in 1984, and Lake Placid in New York in 1980.

Case Study

Chamonix is a winter resort in France. Like most resorts, it has good transportation to large cities and other places where many people live. Some people travel on the regular flights to the airports near Chamonix. Others take trains, including overnight sleepers. It is easy for people from Paris, Marseille, Lyon, and other French cities to spend their weekends in Chamonix. Winter activities there include skiing, skating, ice hockey, sleigh rides, and curling (a game something like bowling played on ice).

Chamonix is also a vacation spot in the summer. The magnificent mountain scenery appeals to tourists, hikers, and climbers. Many visitors enjoy water sports in the mountain lakes and rivers. They may go fishing, canoeing, kayaking, river rafting, swimming, sailing, and waterskiing. New roads, hotels, and apartment complexes have been built in Chamonix, bringing many new jobs. More local people can now find work in the mountains close to their home.

Geography Detective

What would you want to see and do if you took a trip to Chamonix or to a resort like this closer to your home? When would you want to go? Use an atlas to figure out how long it would take you to get there by car, by train, or by airplane. Make a list of the things you would want to do.

Damaging the Mountains

Many climbers have been killed here on the north face of the Eiger

Railway tunnel

Hotel, restaurant, train station, and scientific research station

Train station

Holes cut in the tunnel's side give a view of the valley

Mountain railway

Winter ski slopes

Wide trails have been made for tourists

Thousands of tourists arrive at this train station each day. They visit the hotels and restaurants.

Industries such as tourism, mining, and forestry can damage mountain areas. It is hard to know how to protect the mountains from this damage. On the one hand, if no one used the mountains, few people could live and work in these areas. On the

▲ Scheidegg is a tourist resort that lies at 6,762 feet in the Swiss Alps. You can see how tourism has changed the area.

◄ Part of this forest on the coast of Alaska is being completely cleared away. This type of logging, called clearcutting, causes many problems. When all the trees in an area are removed, there are no roots left to anchor the soil. Heavy rains then erode soil from the mountain slopes. Clearcutting also destroys the homes of many birds and animals.

◀ Some mountain areas are being damaged by air pollution. Towns and cities pollute the atmosphere with smoke and fumes from homes, cars, and industries (1). The water vapor in clouds is also polluted (2). It falls as **acid rain** on mountains that may be hundreds of miles away from the towns (3). Acid rain kills plants and wildlife (4), (5).

other hand, if more and more visitors come, more chairlifts, ski runs, hotels, restaurants, roads, parking lots, and gas stations will be built. There will be more workers, who will need houses. As the natural beauty of the mountains is spoiled, visitors will find somewhere else to go.

Geography Detective

Each year more climbers, hikers, and sightseers visit the mountains. And more damage is done to the mountains and to the wildlife living there. How would you try to solve this problem? Discuss this with your friends. Would you build bigger and better tourist centers? Would you try to keep people away from the mountains? What other solutions might there be?

◀ These pine trees in Germany have been damaged by acid rain.

27

Mapwork

This map shows a small section of a mountain area. The largest town here is Mountain Vale, on the Bluey River. Tourists take the mountain railway or the road to visit Corniche City.

1. Use the scale on the map to find:
   a) the distance in a straight line from Mountain Vale to Corniche City;
   b) the distance you would have to travel if you followed the road from Mountain Vale to Corniche City. Use a piece of string or thread to follow all the bends in the road. What difference is there between the distance in a straight line and the distance by road?

2. Use the compass on the map to work out the direction from Mountain Vale to Corniche City. In which direction is the Bluey River flowing? Is it north, south, northwest, or southwest?

3. What recreational activities would you find if you visited this area? Which town or village do you think is the most popular mountain resort in winter?

4. The letters A, B, and C on the map mark three features that are similar to the features shown in the photographs. Name the features you can see at points A, B, and C on the map.

5. What is the highest point in the area covered by the map?

6. Where would you expect to see a U-shaped valley in the area on the map?

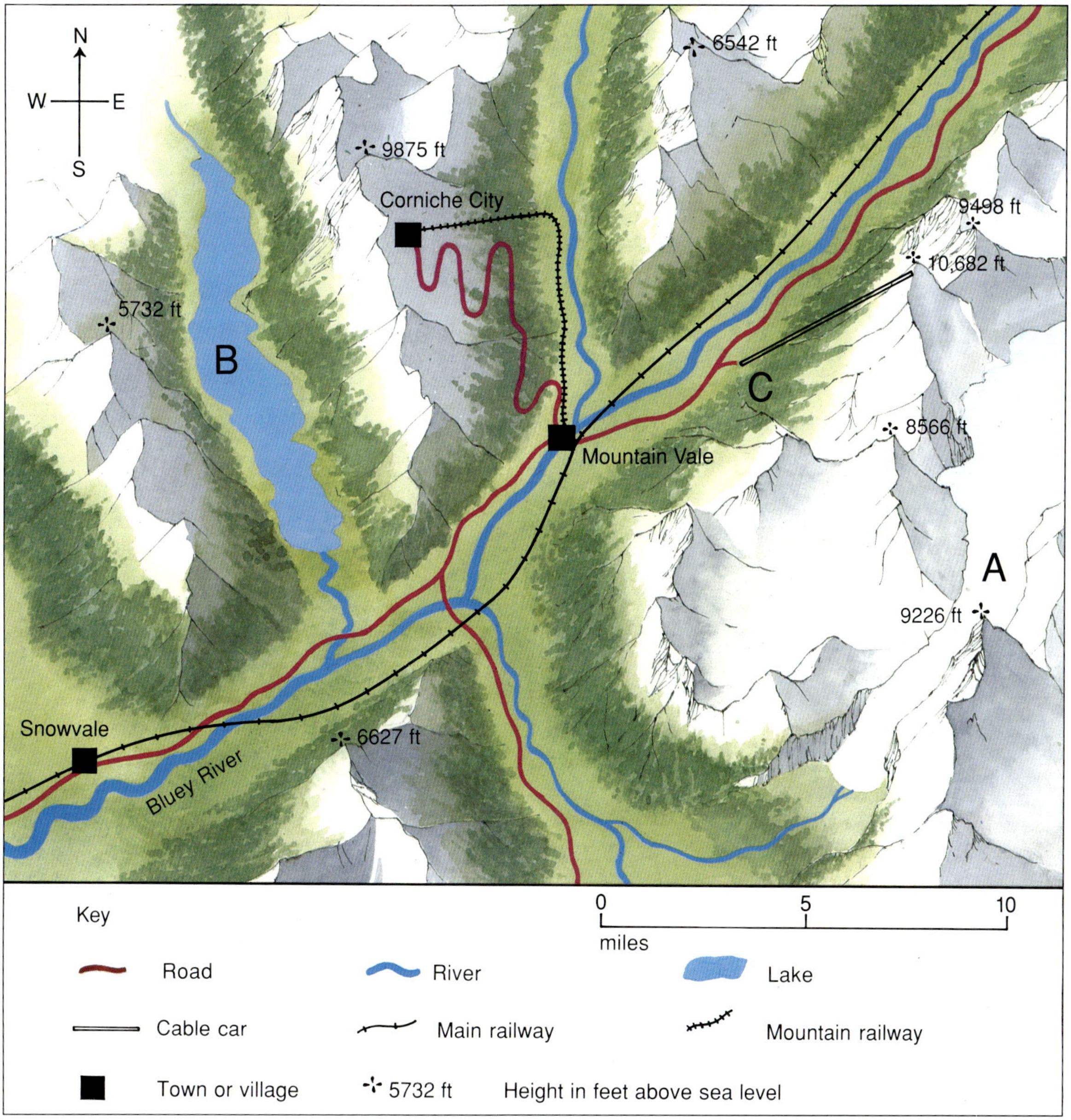

▼ Finger lake

▼ Glacier

▼ Cable car

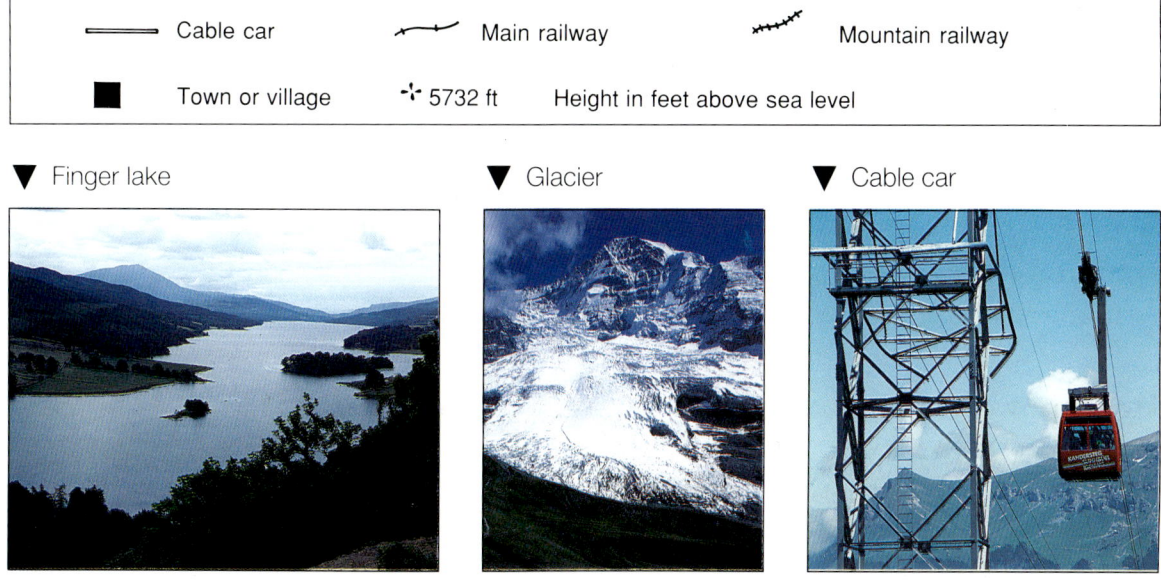

Glossary

acid rain: Rainfall that contains chemical pollutants from the air. When combined with water, these pollutants form acids that can harm plants, animals, and habitats.

Alpines: Small, short-stemmed flowers found above the tree line. They are named after the Alps but are also found in other mountain ranges.

avalanche: A large mass of snow and ice that falls suddenly down a mountainside.

cirque: A deep, rounded hollow with steep sides found high on a mountain.

crevasse: A deep crack in the surface of a glacier.

earthquake: A shaking of the ground, caused by shifting of the earth's crust along a fault or where two plates meet. Volcanic eruptions also can cause earthquakes.

equator: The imaginary line drawn on maps around the center of the earth.

erosion: The wearing away of the earth's surface by water, ice, or wind.

erratic: A boulder carried (sometimes far) from its source by a glacier. The rock is left stranded when the ice melts.

fault: A crack in the earth's surface along which movements from earthquakes and volcanoes take place.

finger lake: A long, narrow lake formed when meltwater from a glacier fills a hollow scooped out by a glacier. A finger lake may also form when moraines block the water's path to the sea.

fold mountains: Mountains formed when earth movements cause the earth's crust to twist or fold over.

foothills: A hilly region at the base of a mountain range.

glacier: A river of ice that moves slowly down a mountainside.

gradient: The steepness of a slope.

hanging valley: A valley that enters a larger valley high up on the wall of the main valley. If the hanging valley has a stream, a waterfall forms where the two valleys meet.

hydropower: Electricity produced from waterpower. Also called hydroelectric power.

ice age: A long cold period when ice sheets cover much of the earth. The last Ice Age ended about 10,000 years ago.

ice sheet: A vast, flat mass of ice and snow covering a large area.

moraine: A mound of soil, gravel, and rocks carried by a glacier and left behind when the ice melts.

plate: A massive slab of the earth's crust.

reservoir: A lake that is formed when a dam is built across a river.

sea level: The surface of the sea, from which the height of the land is measured.

snow line: The height on a mountain slope above which there is always snow or ice.

snowshed: A long shelter that protects a mountain railway or road from avalanches or drifting snow.

striations: Deep scratches or grooves in bare rock caused when the underside of a glacier drags sharp stones across the surface of the rock.

transhumance: The movement of livestock from mountain pastures in the summer to valley pastures in the winter.

tree line: The height on a mountain slope above which no trees will grow.

U-shaped valley: The shape of a valley after it has been eroded by a glacier.

volcanic eruption: The venting of melted rock (lava) through a crack in the earth's crust. Some eruptions are explosive, throwing clouds of gases, ash, and rock into the air.

METRIC CONVERSION CHART		
WHEN YOU KNOW	**MULTIPLY BY**	**TO FIND**
inches	25.4	millimeters
inches	2.54	centimeters
feet	0.3048	meters
miles	1.609	kilometers
square miles	2.59	square kilometers
acres	0.4047	hectares
gallons	3.78	liters
degrees Fahrenheit	.56 (after subtracting 32)	degrees Celsius

Index

acid rain 27
Africa 12, 14
Alaska 8, 9, 26
Alps 6, 9, 13, 18, 20, 26
altitude 22
Andes 6, 16, 18, 22, 23
Asia 4, 5, 6
avalanche 16, 17

chalet 13
Chamonix 25
cirque 11
crevasse 8, 9, 16

earthquakes 6, 7
erosion 22, 26
erratic 9, 11
Europe 4, 5, 6, 10, 20, 25
Everest, Mount 4, 5, 24

farming 20, 22, 23
fault 6, 7
finger lake 11
fold mountains 6
forestry 20, 26

glacier 8, 9, 10, 11, 14, 21
gradient 19

hang gliding 24
hanging valley 10
Himalaya 4, 5, 6, 9, 12, 14, 18, 22
hot-air ballooning 24
hydropower 21

Ice Age 10, 11
ice sheet 8, 10, 11
industry 27

Karakoram 4, 5
Kilimanjaro 12, 14

land use 12
llama 22, 23

meltwater 8
minerals 20
mining 20, 26
moraine 9, 11
mountain range 4

natural resources 20, 21
Nepal 4, 5, 24
North America 4, 5, 7, 9, 10, 11, 20

peak 5
plant life 13, 14, 15, 27
plates 6, 7
pollution 27
Pyrenees 5, 6, 18

railways 17, 18, 19, 28
Rockies 6, 18, 20

San Andreas Fault 7
skiing 17, 24, 25
snow line 13
snowshed 17
South America 6, 7
St. Helens, Mount 7
striations 11
summit 5, 8, 11, 14, 16

temperature 13
terrace 22
tourism 20, 24, 25, 26, 27, 28
transhumance 22
tree line 13, 22

U-shaped valley 10, 11, 28

volcanoes 6, 7

weather 8, 9, 10, 11, 12, 13, 15, 16
wildlife 14, 15, 21, 27
Winter Olympics 25

yaks 18, 22
Y-junction 19